AARDVARKS
CERDOS HORMIGUEROS

Maddie Gibbs

Traducción al español: Eduardo Alamán

PowerKiDS press

New York

For my mom and other garnfark appreciators

Published in 2011 by The Rosen Publishing Group, Inc.
29 East 21st Street, New York, NY 10010

First Edition

Editor: Amelie von Zumbusch
Layout Design: Greg Tucker

Traducción al español: Eduardo Alamán

Photo Credits: Cover Berndt Fischer/Getty Images; p. 5 Joel Sartore/Getty Images; pp. 7, 15, 20–21 Nigel Dennis/Getty Images; pp. 9, 24 (bottom left) Doug Cheeseman/Peter Arnold, Inc.; pp. 11, 24 (top right) © Nigel Dennis/age fotostock; pp. 13, 24 (top left) Alan Root/Getty Images; pp. 17, 24 (bottom right) © Alan Root/ Peter Arnold, Inc.; p. 19 Anthony Bannister/Getty Images; p.22–23 © APA/ Peter Arnold, Inc.

Library of Congress Cataloging-in-Publication Data

Gibbs, Maddie.
[Aardvarks. Spanish & English]
Aardvarks = Cerdos hormigueros / by Maddie Gibbs. — 1st ed.
p. cm. — (Safari animals = Animales de safari) Includes index.
ISBN 978-1-4488-3214-9 (library binding)
1. Aardvark—Juvenile literature. I. Title. II. Title: Cerdos hormigueros.
QL737.T8G5318 2011
599.3′1—dc22

2010026004

Manufactured in the United States of America

CPSIA Compliance Information: Batch #WW11PK: For Further Information contact Rosen Publishing, New York, New York at 1-800-237-9932

Web Sites: Due to the changing nature of Internet links, PowerKids Press has developed an online list of Web sites related to the subject of this book. This site is updated regularly. Please use this link to access the list: www.powerkidslinks.com/safari/aard/

Contents

Contenido

This strange-looking animal is an aardvark.

Este animal de raro aspecto es un cerdo hormiguero.

Aardvarks live in Africa. They can be found in both forests and grasslands.

Los cerdos hormigueros viven en África. Los cerdos hormigueros viven en bosques y praderas.

Aardvarks have long **snouts**. They have big ears, too.

Los cerdos hormigueros tiene largos **hocicos**. Además tienen orejas grandes.

Aardvarks have sharp **claws**. Their claws make them very good at digging.

Los cerdos hormigueros tienen **garras** filosas. Estas garras son muy buenas para escavar.

11

Aardvarks dig **burrows**. They most often sleep in their burrows during the day.

Los cerdos hormigueros escavan **madrigueras**. Generalmente duermen en sus madrigueras durante el día.

13

In the evening, aardvarks leave their burrows to look for food.

Por la noche, los cerdos hormigueros salen de sus madrigueras a buscar comida.

Aardvarks often break open **termite mounds** to suck out the termites.

Con frecuencia, los cerdos hormigueros hacen hoyos en los **nidos de las termitas** para alimentarse de estos insectos.

Aardvarks dig up ants, too. They eat around 50,000 insects each night!

Los cerdos hormigueros también comen hormigas. ¡Los cerdos hormigueros comen unos 50,000 insectos cada noche!

Most of the time,
aardvarks live
by themselves.

Los cerdos
hormigueros viven
solos la mayoría
del tiempo.

However, baby aardvarks live with their mothers.

Sin embargo, los bebés viven con sus mamás.

23

Words to Know / Palabras que debes saber

burrow/(la) madriguera

claw/(la) garra

snout/(el) hocico

termite mound/
(el) nidos de termitas

Index

Índice